I am the hero of my own life.

A GUIDED JOURNAL BY BRIANNA WIEST

THOUGHT
CATALOG
Books

This book was designed by KJ Parish and published by Thought Catalog Books, a publishing house owned by The Thought & Expression Company. It was printed in 2018 and was published in an edition of 2,000 copies.

ISBN 978-0-9964871-8-4

10 9 8 7 6 5 4 3

The title of this book is an answer to Swami Chetanananda's *Will I Be the Hero of My Own Life?* It's not just a yes, but a how. Every important story we tell, every lesson learned, everything that has changed and shaped and opened us ultimately shows us one thing: that we are here to save ourselves. We are tasked to become the god we have been praying to, the love we have been waiting for, the partner we dreamed of marrying. We are not only required to do this; we are destined to. Our desires and our pain are a blueprint of what we are here to do. This is the revelation: You already have everything you want. You already are everything you aspire to be. Your fate is the opposite of your fears. This book is not about healing, it is about realizing you are already healed and watching everything fall into place on its own.

This is
your life.

You are
responsible for it.

That which you sow
you shall also reap.

That which you
believe you shall
also live.

This is your life. You are the only one who decides how it goes. You are the only one who can give yourself the joy, the hope, the love, the money, the experiences, and the existence you crave. You are not stuck; you only think you are stuck. You are not broken; you only think you are broken. Healing is the process of remembering you are still okay and always were. This is your life. You are the only one who has to live it. Everything you judge, everything you see, everything you interpret, everything you fear is all a projection. This is your life. And if you want to change it, the first step is realizing that you've had the power all along. The first step is saying: *I am willing to see this change.*

I AM WILLING

I am willing to see _____ change.

I am willing to see _____ blossom.

I am willing to see _____ grow.

I am willing to see _____ die.

I am willing to see _____ be transformed.

I am willing to see _____ come back to life.

I am willing to see _____ differently.

I am willing to see _____ forgiven.

I am willing to see _____ better than I hoped.

I am willing to see _____ greater than I dreamed.

I am willing to see _____ with humility.

I am willing to see _____ released.

I am willing to see _____ improve.

I am willing to see _____ reinvented.

I am willing to see _____ believed.

I am willing to see _____ changed forever.

All of the things I thought I'd *never* get over
and then one day did:

LIST

This is what I'd tell my younger self
if I could speak with them now:

_____

_____

_____

_____

_____

_____

_____

_____

_____

_____

_____

_____

_____

_____

_____

_____

_____

_____

LIST

This is who I would be without my pain narrative.
This is who I would be without my struggle:

INTERSECTIONS

A Personal Venn Diagram

Complete the following three lists to explore what you like, what you are good at, and what the world needs. Then, consider how and where these three areas intersect or overlap.

This Is What
I'm Good At

_____

_____

_____

_____

_____

_____

_____

_____

_____

_____

_____

_____

_____

This Is
What I Like

This is What
The World Needs

This Is Where
All Of These Intersect

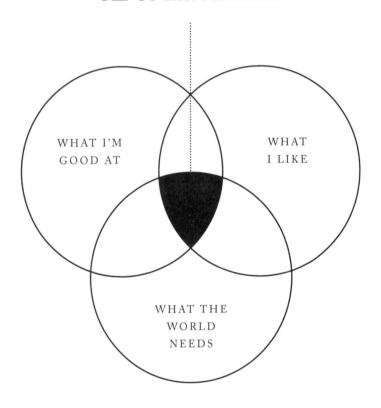

GRATITUDE

Thank you, thank you, thank you for:

_____

_____

_____

(thing you are struggling with most)

I understand that this is imperative to my growth. I understand that my fear is trying to keep me safe.

Thank you, thank you, thank you, for:

_____

_____

_____

(thing that has caused you pain)

I understand that this has manifested in order to make me better.

Thank you, thank you, thank you for:

_____

_____

_____

(uncomfortable feeling that keeps coming up)

I understand that I am becoming aware of it so that I can change the pattern in my life. Thank you, thank you, thank you for all of the things that have been going so well in my life, that have reminded me hope is still here. Thank you, thank you, thank you for all of the things that I wish were going better, that have reminded me I am meant to make them that way. In being grateful, I am no longer resisting it. When I no longer resist it, it no longer has a hold over me.

LIST

If I had to leave tomorrow with only the belongings
I could fit into my car to retreat to a desert island
where nobody would hear from me again…

I would take these things:

_____

_____

_____

_____

_____

_____

_____

_____

_____

_____

_____

_____

_____

_____

_____

I would take these people:

_____

_____

_____

_____

_____

_____

_____

_____

_____

_____

_____

_____

_____

_____

_____

_____

_____

_____

_____

_____

I would do this each day:

_____

_____

_____

_____

_____

_____

_____

_____

_____

_____

_____

_____

_____

_____

_____

_____

_____

_____

LIST

These are the things that bother me
most about other people:

_____

_____

_____

_____

_____

_____

_____

_____

_____

_____

_____

_____

_____

_____

_____

_____

_____

These are the things I don't like
to admit that I dislike about myself:

_____

_____

_____

_____

_____

_____

_____

_____

_____

_____

_____

_____

_____

_____

_____

_____

LIST

These are the things I love about other people:

_____

_____

_____

_____

_____

_____

_____

_____

_____

_____

_____

_____

_____

_____

_____

_____

These are the things I love about myself:

_____

_____

_____

_____

_____

_____

_____

_____

_____

_____

_____

_____

_____

_____

_____

_____

LIST

If social media didn't exist,
here's how I would live differently:

_____

_____

_____

_____

_____

_____

_____

_____

_____

_____

_____

_____

"Instead of worrying I am being tricked by a medicine you take once and then are magically healed by, I can consider that gardens require maintenance. Fallible human beings require maintenance. There is weeding and watering to be done every day, and there's never a point where you are done working and your garden suddenly takes care of itself."

—*Chrissy Stockton*

LIST

These are the qualities of the person
I always wished I'd marry:

_____

_____

_____

_____

_____

_____

_____

_____

_____

_____

_____

_____

_____

_____

_____

_____

This is how <u>I</u> am going to become that person instead:

On the days of my life that I can recall being happiest,
this is what I was doing:

LIST

If my fears were actually symbols for my desires,
this is what I would be trying to tell myself:

_____

_____

_____

_____

_____

_____

_____

_____

_____

_____

_____

_____

_____

_____

_____

LIST

If I knew beyond a shadow of a doubt that I was the one in control of my life and I could create absolutely anything I wanted, this is what I would change:

_____

_____

_____

_____

_____

_____

_____

_____

_____

_____

_____

_____

_____

DRAW

This is what I think my true self looks like ——→

(a self-portait)

LIST

Imagine yourself in five years. Imagine meeting that person and having a conversation with them.

What do they look like?
What do they tell you?
How do they feel?

DRAW AND EXAMINE

What are the things you dream of for your life?

Got them? Okay, now draw them in this space ⟶

Now cross out anything that's physical.

Money, a better body, a new car or house or anything like that.

Is there anything left?

If so, what is it?

If not, why?

"It is not the critic who counts; not the man who points out how the strong man stumbles, or where the doer of deeds could have done them better. The credit belongs to the man who is actually in the arena, whose face is marred by dust and sweat and blood, who strives valiantly, who errs, who comes short again and again, because there is no effort without error and shortcoming; but who does actually strive to do the deeds, who knows great enthusiasms, the great devotions, who spends himself in a worthy cause, who at the best knows in the end the triumph of high achievement, and who at the worst, if he fails, at least fails while daring greatly, so that his place shall never be with those cold and timid souls who neither know victory nor defeat."

—*Angela Duckworth*

PRAYER

These are the most powerful prayers in the universe,
and you say them all the time:

I am thankful for…
I am grateful for…
I am sick of…
I am worried about…
I am…

Stop trying to let go. Stop trying to push away. The sheer force of you trying to ignore something spotlights your attention on it. Stop standing in the ruins. Build the new city. What is the opposite of everything you fear and feel? What would stand in place of everything you're trying to "let go" of? Run to it. Become it. Think about nothing but it. Soon it will become you, too.

PHOTO

Find a photo of yourself from five or more years ago.

Glue it on this page ⟶

Flip back to remember how far you've come.

If you could wake up tomorrow completely healed
and fully the person you want to be,
what would your day look like?

Thank you, thank you, thank you for the anxiety. Thank you for the loss. Thank you for everything I resisted and suppressed. Thank you for the shadows, thank you for the heaviness. Thank you, thank you, thank you. These things are not here to punish me; they are here to transform me. It only hurts when I don't understand their power and their purpose, and therefore, it is with fear that I punish myself.

When you've lost your trust in the universe, when you don't feel like you can relax into life because it hasn't supported you before, remember this: your setup is probably wrong. You're thinking that there's you, and then there's this singular "god," a separate entity that may or may not grace you. In reality, you are part of the whole energy field and life supports life. Mother Nature wants everything to thrive, to grow, to move toward the sun—and you are of this nature. You don't need to beg, pray, or wait for grace, you are it. It is impossible to be unsupported. The leaf that has to wrap around the branch to reach the sun's rays is not being punished, it is being guided and redirected. Life supports life and you are part of life. You can relax knowing that your growth, your joy, your grace, your calm, your vision serves everything and everyone because it is part of everything and everyone. You do not need trust. You only have to know.

The oak doesn't contemplate shedding leaves and deepening roots. The evergreen does not require effort to hold onto its needles. You are the only one capable of mourning the leaves and wondering about the trees. You are only in pain because you are trying to resist what you are. The thing about your nature is that she isn't stasis. We use that term to describe that within us which is unchangeable—but that's not what nature is at all. She has cycles and patterns, she has traits and reactions. But she isn't predictable. She evolves—she must. And so does everything she touches.

I am better than I have ever been.

Every day, in every way, I am getting better and better.

I am healthier than I have ever been.

I am in a better financial position than I have ever been.

I have better friends than I have ever had.

I am happier with my life than I have ever been.

I am growing and improving every day.

I can look back on my life and I see how far I've come.

I can look at my life now and see where I want to go.

I am healed and know now that I always have been.

I am whole and know now that I always have been.

I am happy and know now that I have always been.

I have the power to create the life I want. I am the one I have been waiting for all along. I am the spouse, the god, the healing, and the wholeness. It has been me all along. I can create exactly what I want—no, not the money, or the job, or the status, but the inner peace, and the awe, and the joy, and the love. You know, the good stuff.

LIST

This is a list of things I find very, very beautiful:

_____

_____

_____

_____

_____

_____

_____

_____

_____

_____

_____

_____

_____

To honor the mind's power, put it to work. Let it remind you to drink water, pay your bills, stay organized, clean the house when it's time. Let your mind be your yang, your masculine force. Let it tell you *how*.

To honor the soul's power, put it to work. Let it tell you whom to spend time with. Let it tell you what to do with your days. Let it remind you that the smell of fresh air is the best feeling and that you are destined for more than what you have now. Let your soul be your yin, your feminine force. Let it tell you *what*.

LIST

Here is a list of small changes I could start making each
day that would ultimately help me reach my biggest goals:

_____

_____

_____

_____

_____

_____

_____

_____

_____

_____

_____

_____

_____

_____

Describe your best self.

Your calmest, most patient, most relaxed, most knowing, most wise, most accepting, most happy self. Not your most successful or glamorous self: that's your ego's best self. The real you. The one that's trying to emerge.

LIST

Ask someone close to you to describe you and your life as though you were trying to explain yourself to a stranger. Write or paste what they say here.

$$\downarrow$$

_____

_____

_____

_____

_____

_____

_____

_____

_____

_____

_____

_____

This is how the world that matters sees you.

LIST

This is the fondest memory I have with my parents:

_____

_____

_____

_____

_____

_____

_____

_____

_____

_____

_____

_____

_____

_____

_____

This is the time in my life in which I felt most like myself:

_____

_____

_____

_____

_____

_____

_____

_____

_____

_____

_____

_____

_____

_____

_____

_____

"Start with this: not all pain matters. There are people whose attention is consistently drawn away from their purpose and toward their pain, like a moth to a light. Such people, who pay attention to every annoyance and obstacle in their way, are usually unsuccessful in their endeavors. In extreme cases they are mentally ill. A healthy person, a flourishing person, learns to move past a lot of annoyance and a good deal of pain.

—*Eric Greitens*

16 Uncomfortable Feelings That Actually Indicate You're On The Right Path

Discomfort is what happens when we are on the precipice of change. Unfortunately, we often confuse it for unhappiness and cope with the latter while running from the former. It usually takes a bit of discomfort to break through to a new understanding, to release a limiting belief, to motivate ourselves to create real change. Discomfort is a signal, one that is often very helpful.

Here are a few (less than desirable) feelings that may indicate you're on the right path after all:

1. Feeling as though you are reliving your childhood struggles.
You find that you're seeing issues you struggled with as a kid reappear in your adult life, and while on the surface this may seem like a matter of not having overcome them, it really means you are becoming conscious of why you think and feel so you can change it.

2. Feeling "lost" or directionless.
Feeling lost is actually a sign you're becoming more present in your life—you're living less within the narratives and ideas that you premeditated and more in the moment at hand. Until you're used to this, it will feel as though you're off track (you aren't).

3. "Left brain" fogginess.
When you're utilizing the right hemisphere more often (you're becoming more intuitive, you're dealing with emotions, you're creating), sometimes it can seem as though "left brain" functions leave you feeling fuzzy. Things such as focusing, organizing, and remembering small details suddenly become difficult.

4. Having random influxes of irrational anger or sadness that intensify until you can't ignore them anymore.

When emotions erupt it's usually because they're "coming up" to be recognized, and our job is to learn to stop grappling with them or resisting them and to simply become fully conscious of them. (After that we control them, not the opposite way around.)

5. Experiencing unpredictable and scattered sleeping patterns.

You'll need to sleep a lot more or a lot less. You'll wake up in the middle of the night because you can't stop thinking about something. You find yourself full of energy or completely exhausted and with little in between.

6. A life-changing event is taking place or just has.

You suddenly having to move, getting divorced, losing a job, having a car break down, etc.

7. Having an intense need to be alone.

You're suddenly disenchanted with the idea of spending every weekend out socializing, and other people's problems are draining you more than they are intriguing you. This means you're recalibrating.

8. Intense, vivid dreaming that you almost always remember in detail.

If dreams are how your subconscious mind communicates with you (or projects an image of your experience), then yours are definitely trying to say something. You're having dreams at an intensity that you've never experienced before.

9. Downsizing your friend group; feeling more and more uncomfortable around negative people.
The thing about negative people is that they rarely realize they are negative, and because you feel uncomfortable saying anything (and you're even more uncomfortable keeping that in your life), you're ghosting a bit on old friends.

10. Feeling like the dreams you had for your life are collapsing.
What you do not realize at this moment is that it is making way for a reality better than you could have thought of, one that's more aligned with who you are, not who you thought you would be.

11. Feeling as though your worst enemy is your thoughts.
You're beginning to realize that your thoughts do create your experience, and it's often not until we're pushed to our wit's end that we even try to take control of them—and that's when we realize that we were in control all along.

12. Feeling unsure of who you really are.
Your past illusions about who you "should" be are dissolving. You feel unsure because it is uncertain! You're in the process of evolving, and we don't become uncertain when we change for the worse (we become angry and closed off). In other words: If what you're experiencing is insecurity or uncertainty, it's usually going to lead to something better.

13. Recognizing how far you still have to go.
When you realize this, it's because you can also see where you're headed; it means you finally know where and who you want to be.

14. "Knowing" things you don't want to know.

Such as what someone is really feeling, or that a relationship isn't going to last, or that you won't be at your job much longer. A lot of "irrational" anxiety comes from subconsciously sensing something, yet not taking it seriously because it isn't logical.

15. Having a radically intense desire to speak up for yourself.

Becoming angry with how much you've let yourself be walked on or how much you've let other people's voices get into your head is a sign that you're finally ready to stop listening and love yourself by respecting yourself first.

16. Realizing you are the only person responsible for your life and your happiness.

This kind of emotional autonomy is terrifying, because it means that if you mess up, it's all on you. At the same time, realizing it is the only way to be truly free. The risk is worth the reward on this one, always.

ABOUT ME

This is my favorite color to wear:

_____

This is my coffee order:

_____

This is my favorite place I've visited:

_____

This is my favorite flower:

_____

This is my ideal weekend:

_____

_____

_____

This is what I like to do on my own:

_____

_____

This is someone I love a lot:

_____

This is what I hope to accomplish in my life:

_____

_____

_____

This is what unnerves me most about the world:

_____

_____

This is a quote that inspires me:

_____

_____

This is a person I look up to:

_____

This is a secret pleasure I don't admit to:

_____

_____

This is my favorite day of the week:

_____

This is my zodiac sign:

_____

This is my best friend's name:

_____

This is my home:

_____

_____

_____

If I could completely remove one memory from my life,
it would be this one:

_____

_____

_____

_____

_____

_____

_____

_____

_____

_____

_____

_____

_____

_____

If I could redo the last five years,
here's what I'd do differently:

LIST

These are the most important lessons
I've learned in the past five years:

_____

_____

_____

_____

_____

_____

_____

_____

_____

_____

_____

_____

_____

_____

_____

_____

_____

LIST

This is what has significantly changed
about my personality in the past five years:

_____

_____

_____

_____

_____

_____

_____

_____

_____

_____

_____

_____

_____

_____

_____

_____

LIST

If I could change anything about human nature,
this is what I would change:

_____

_____

_____

_____

_____

_____

_____

_____

_____

_____

_____

_____

_____

_____

LIST

This is a recurring theme
that I experience regularly in my dreams:

_____

_____

_____

_____

_____

_____

_____

_____

_____

_____

_____

_____

LIST

This is where I'd travel if I could work remotely
and had free airfare for life:

_____

_____

_____

_____

_____

_____

_____

_____

_____

_____

_____

_____

_____

_____

These are the things I now have in my life that I once
only could have dreamed of:

_____

_____

_____

_____

_____

_____

_____

_____

_____

_____

_____

_____

_____

_____

_____

_____

_____

LIST

These are the ways in which my life turned out better
than I anticipated it would:

_____

_____

_____

_____

_____

_____

_____

_____

_____

_____

_____

_____

_____

_____

_____

_____

_____

"I never change, I simply become more myself."

—*Joyce Carol Oates*

"One day, after all, you will be dead. Then you will be in the ground. You will buy no more flowers or pretty dresses, you will take no more vacations, or spend money on anything else. So if there is something that will brighten your day, do it now. Defy death. Revel in this brief moment, here, in this world full of intermittent beauty."

—*Jennifer Wright*

This is what I believe is worth suffering for:

LIST

This is the advice that once helped me
through a really tough time:

_____

_____

_____

_____

_____

_____

_____

_____

_____

_____

_____

_____

_____

_____

LIST

This is what I will spend my days thinking about
when I am fully healed and happy:

_____

_____

_____

_____

_____

_____

This is what I will spend my days doing
when I am fully healed and happy:

_____

_____

_____

_____

_____

This is how I will think about the things that challenge
me when I am fully healed and happy:

Everything you dream you will do, could do, might do when you are better...everything you hope that will transpire into your being by the virtue of your outside world changing...those things are not your rewards, they are your tools. Do them now. Think them now. Be them now. Life unfolds from the inside out.

"Everybody has a little bit of the sun and moon in them. Everybody has a little bit of man, woman, and animal in them. Darks and lights in them. Everyone is part of a connected cosmic system. Part earth and sea, wind and fire, with some salt and dust swimming in them. We have a universe within ourselves that mimics the universe outside. None of us are just black or white, or never wrong and always right. No one. No one exists without polarities. Everybody has good and bad forces working with them, against them, and within them."

—*Suzy Kassem*

LIST

This is a thank you letter to someone
who has loved me unconditionally in my life:

_____

_____

_____

_____

_____

_____

_____

_____

_____

_____

_____

_____

_____

_____

This is a thank you letter to my younger self
for getting me to where I am now:

LIST

This is an apology letter to my younger self
for all of the times I was so mean to myself:

_____

_____

_____

_____

_____

_____

_____

_____

_____

_____

_____

_____

_____

_____

LIST

This is where I hope to be in five years:

_____

_____

_____

_____

_____

_____

_____

_____

_____

_____

_____

_____

_____

_____

LIST

These are the 10 things I do
most frequently on any typical day:

1

2

3

4

5

6

7

8

9

10

LIST

This is where I will *actually* be in five years
if my daily habits stay the same:

It is not whether you take time to go outside, but whether you can sit outside and do nothing else but breathe in life and just enjoy it. That is the mark of having made it somewhere worth going.

LIST

These are the things I most commonly crave:

_____

_____

_____

_____

_____

_____

_____

_____

_____

_____

_____

_____

_____

_____

_____

_____

LIST

This is what those cravings are
emotional representations of:

_____

_____

_____

_____

_____

_____

_____

_____

_____

_____

_____

_____

_____

_____

_____

_____

20 Signs You're Doing Better Than You Think You Are

1. You paid the bills this month and maybe even had extra to spend on non-necessities. It doesn't matter how much you belabored the checks as they went out; the point is that they did, and you figured it out regardless.

2. You question yourself. You doubt your life. You feel miserable some days. This means you're still open to growth. This means you can be objective and self-aware. The best people go home at the end of the day and think: "or...maybe there's another way."

3. You have a job. For however many hours, at whatever rate, you are earning money that helps you eat something, sleep on something, wear something every day. It's not failure if it doesn't look the way you thought it would—you're valuing your independence and taking responsibility for yourself.

4. You have time to do something you enjoy, even if "what you enjoy" is sitting on the couch and ordering dinner and watching Netflix.

5. You are not worried about where your next meal is coming from. There's food in the fridge or pantry, and you have enough to actually pick and choose what you want to eat.

6. You can eat because you enjoy it. It's not a matter of sheer survival.

7. You have one or two truly close friends. People worry about the quantity but eventually tend to realize the number of people you can claim to be in your tribe has no bearing on how much you feel intimacy, acceptance, community, or joy. At the end of the day, all we really want are a few close people who know us (and love us) no matter what.

8. You could afford a subway ride, cup of coffee, or the gas in your car this morning. The smallest conveniences (and oftentimes, necessities) are not variables for you.

You're not the same person you were a year ago. You're learning, and evolving, and can identify the ways in which you've changed for better and worse.

9. You have the time and means to do things beyond the bare minimum. You've maybe been to a concert in the last few years, you buy books for yourself, you could take a day trip to a neighboring city if you wanted—you don't have to work all hours of the day to survive.

10. You have a selection of clothing at your disposal. You aren't worried about having a hat or gloves in a blizzard; you have cool clothes for the summer and something to wear to a wedding.

11. You not only can shield and decorate your body but can do so appropriately for a variety of circumstances.

12. You can sense what isn't right in your life. The first and most crucial step is simply being aware. Being able to communicate to yourself: "Something is not right, even though I am not yet sure what would feel better."

13. If you could talk to your younger self, you would be able to say: "We did it, we made it out, we survived that terrible thing." So often people carry their past traumas into their present lives, and if you want any proof that we carry who we were in who we are, all you need to do is see how you respond to your inner child hearing

"you're going to be okay" from the person you became.

14. You have a space of your own. It doesn't even have to be a home or apartment (but that's great if it is). All you need is a room, a corner, a desk, where you can create or rest at your discretion; where you govern who gets to be part of your weird little world and to what capacity. It's one of the few controls we can actually exert.

15. You've lost relationships. More important than the fact that you've simply had them in the first place is that you or your former partner chose not to settle. You opened yourself to the possibility of something else being out there.

16. You're interested in something, whether it's how to live a happier life, maintain better relationships, reading or movies or sex or society or the axis on which the world spins, something intrigues you to explore it.

17. You know how to take care of yourself. You know how many hours of sleep you need to feel okay the next day, who to turn to when you're heartbroken, what you have fun doing, what to do when you don't feel well, etc.

18. You're working toward a goal. Even if you're exhausted and it feels miles away, you have a dream for yourself, however vague and malleable.

19. But you're not uncompromisingly set on anything for your future. Some of the happiest and best adjusted people are the ones who can make any situation an ideal, who are too immersed in the moment to intricately plan and decidedly commit to any one specific outcome.

20. You've been through some crap. You can look at challenges you currently face and compare them to ones you thought you'd never get over. You can reassure yourself through your own experience. Life did not get easier; you got smarter.

LIST

If I were to describe my life to a stranger,
this is what I would say about it:

_____

_____

_____

_____

_____

_____

_____

_____

_____

_____

_____

_____

_____

_____

When I describe my life to my best friend,
this is what I say about it:

_____

_____

_____

_____

_____

_____

_____

_____

_____

_____

_____

_____

_____

_____

_____

_____

_____

LIST

This is how I'm being dishonest with myself
about how I really feel about my life:

_____

_____

_____

_____

_____

_____

_____

_____

_____

_____

_____

_____

_____

"If you want to see what you're truly committed to, look at your results."

—*Jennifer Ho-Dougatz*

LIST

If I knew everybody would agree with me,
these are the opinions I'd be more open about:

LIST

If I knew that everybody would support me,
here's how I'd live my life differently:

_____

_____

_____

_____

_____

_____

_____

_____

_____

_____

_____

_____

_____

_____

LIST

These are a few things I can admit I was wrong about,
but now know better:

_____

_____

_____

_____

_____

_____

_____

_____

_____

_____

_____

_____

_____

_____

_____

_____

_____

LIST

These are the relationships that have meant
the most to me in my life:

_____

_____

_____

_____

_____

_____

_____

_____

_____

_____

_____

_____

_____

_____

LIST

These are the things those relationships have in common:

"There's an old saying in neuroscience: neurons that fire together wire together. This means the more you run a neuro-circuit in your brain, the stronger that circuit becomes. This is why, to quote another old saw, practice makes perfect. The more you practice piano, or speaking a language, or juggling, the stronger those circuits get. The ability to learn is about more than building and strengthening neural connections. For years this has been the focus for learning new things. But as it turns out, the ability to learn is about more than building and strengthening neural connections. Even more important is our ability to break down the old ones. It's called "synaptic pruning."

—*Judah Pollack*

These are a few ways I am aware that I self-sabotage:

LIST

These are a few reasons why I think I self-sabotage:

_____

_____

_____

_____

_____

_____

_____

_____

_____

_____

_____

_____

_____

_____

_____

LIST

This is what I would define as my comfort zone:

This is what I would be willing to step out of it to achieve:

_____

_____

_____

_____

_____

_____

_____

_____

_____

_____

_____

_____

_____

_____

Everything you have written in these pages, you already knew. Every time you read something that made you feel like everything was beautiful and all of the loose ends seemed to finally tie up in your mind—that was your soul talking. It was saying yes, I told you.

Your feelings are always valid; they are very often not real. You cannot bring chaos into your life by worrying. Worrying attracts more worrying, not more trauma. You can, however, rob yourself of your best years with the illusion that the worrying keeps you safe. It doesn't. We will be temporarily screwed at some points and end up okay in the end…whether we worry or not.

If someone says they don't want a relationship, believe them. If you do your best and work your hardest and don't get anywhere, try heading somewhere else. You don't have to work hard; your purpose will feel effortless.

It will require dedication, which should also feel pretty innate. Anything else you do to generate tension and chaos is a way to disconnect from yourself. Your ongoing problems aren't problems, they are loves. You can't let them go because they serve you in some way you don't consciously recognize. Figure out what need they are feeding, and they'll dissolve effortlessly.

Your whole life is an unfolding. It's not about finally getting to where you want to be but realizing you have always been there. It is realizing you are already the person you dream of, you already have the power you crave, the happiness that you've been waiting for has been in front of you the whole time, and the life you've dreamed of was accessible from the moment you conceived of it.

It was only you that was holding you back.

BRIANNA WIEST is a writer, author, and editor. She has published thousands of articles that have been read by millions of people throughout the world. She currently works for a variety of national publications. This is her fifth book published by Thought Catalog Books.

For more information, or to book Brianna for writing or speaking engagements, please visit briannawiest.com.

THOUGHT
CATALOG
Books

Thought Catalog Books is a publishing house owned by The Thought & Expression Company, an independent media group based in Brooklyn, NY. Founded in 2010, we are committed to facilitating thought and expression. We exist to help people become better communicators and listeners in order to engender a more exciting, attentive, and imaginative world. We are powered by Collective World, a community of creatives and writers from all over the globe.

Visit us at *www.thoughtcatalogbooks.com* and *www.collective.world*.